50 Irish Pub Favorite Recipes for Home

By: Kelly Johnson

Table of Contents

- Irish Stew
- Fish and Chips
- Shepherd's Pie
- Bangers and Mash
- Dublin Coddle
- Boxty
- Irish Soda Bread
- Corned Beef and Cabbage
- Guinness Beef Stew
- Irish Coffee
- Colcannon
- Irish Lamb Pie
- Irish Potato Soup
- Irish Cheddar and Ale Soup
- Black Pudding
- Dublin Lawyer
- Irish Apple Cake
- Irish Whiskey Trifle
- Irish Boxty Pancakes
- Colcannon Soup
- Beef and Guinness Pie
- Irish Seafood Chowder
- Beef and Mushroom Boxty
- Irish Bacon and Cabbage
- Traditional Irish Breakfast
- Dubliner Cheese Dip
- Irish Chicken Pot Pie
- Whiskey Glazed Salmon
- Irish Nachos
- Potato Leek Soup
- Irish Cream Cheesecake
- Steak and Guinness Pie
- Irish Lamb Stew
- Irish Coffee Chocolate Mousse
- Dubliner Cheese and Bacon Dip

- Irish Smoked Salmon Boxty
- Irish Cream Bread Pudding
- Irish Whiskey Cake
- Dubliner Cheese and Onion Tart
- Irish Stout Ice Cream
- Potato and Leek Boxty
- Baileys Irish Cream Cheesecake
- Dubliner Cheese and Herb Scones
- Irish Whiskey Truffles
- Irish Potato Boxty
- Irish Cream Chocolate Tart
- Dubliner Cheese and Bacon Scones
- Irish Cream Tiramisu
- Whiskey Glazed Chicken Wings
- Irish Coffee Panna Cotta

Irish Stew

Ingredients:

- 1.5 kg (3.3 lbs) lamb shoulder, cut into chunks
- 4 large potatoes, peeled and cut into chunks
- 3 carrots, peeled and sliced
- 3 onions, peeled and sliced
- 2 tablespoons vegetable oil
- 3 tablespoons all-purpose flour
- 1 liter (4 cups) beef or lamb broth
- 2-3 sprigs of fresh thyme (or 1 teaspoon dried thyme)
- 2 bay leaves
- Salt and pepper to taste
- Chopped fresh parsley for garnish (optional)

Instructions:

In a large pot, heat the vegetable oil over medium-high heat.
Toss the lamb chunks in flour, seasoned with salt and pepper.
Brown the lamb pieces in the pot until they are golden on all sides. Work in batches to avoid overcrowding the pot.
Once the lamb is browned, remove it from the pot and set it aside.
In the same pot, add a bit more oil if needed, and sauté the sliced onions until they are soft and translucent.
Return the browned lamb to the pot and add the potatoes and carrots.
Pour in the beef or lamb broth to cover the ingredients. Add the thyme and bay leaves.
Bring the stew to a boil, then reduce the heat to low, cover the pot, and simmer for about 2 hours or until the lamb is tender.
Check the seasoning and adjust with salt and pepper if needed.
Once the stew is cooked, remove the bay leaves and thyme sprigs.
Serve hot, garnished with chopped fresh parsley if desired.

Irish Stew is often enjoyed with a slice of crusty bread or traditional Irish soda bread. It's a comforting and satisfying dish, perfect for colder weather or when you're in the mood for a classic Irish meal.

Fish and Chips

Ingredients:

For the Fish:

- 4 fillets of white fish (such as cod or haddock)
- 1 cup all-purpose flour
- 1 cup beer (lager or ale)
- 1 teaspoon baking powder
- Salt and pepper to taste
- Vegetable oil for frying

For the Chips:

- 4 large potatoes, peeled and cut into thick strips
- Vegetable oil for frying
- Salt to taste

Instructions:

For the Fish:

In a mixing bowl, combine the flour, baking powder, salt, and pepper.
Gradually whisk in the beer to create a smooth batter. Let the batter rest for at least 30 minutes.
Heat vegetable oil in a deep fryer or a large, deep pan to 180°C (350°F).
Dip each fish fillet into the batter, ensuring it is fully coated.
Carefully lower the battered fish into the hot oil and fry for about 5-7 minutes or until the fish is golden brown and cooked through.
Remove the fried fish from the oil and place it on a plate lined with paper towels to absorb excess oil.

For the Chips:

In the same hot oil used for the fish, carefully add the potato strips.
Fry the potatoes until they are golden brown and crispy. This may take about 5-8 minutes.

Remove the chips from the oil and place them on a plate lined with paper towels. Season the chips with salt while they are still hot.

Serve:

- Serve the hot and crispy fish alongside the chips.
- Optionally, serve with tartar sauce, malt vinegar, or your preferred dipping sauce.

Fish and Chips is often enjoyed wrapped in newspaper or served on a platter. It's a beloved comfort food that can be enjoyed in a casual setting or as a classic takeaway dish.

Shepherd's Pie

Ingredients:

For the Filling:

- 500g minced lamb or beef
- 1 onion, finely chopped
- 2 carrots, peeled and diced
- 2 cloves garlic, minced
- 2 tablespoons tomato paste
- 2 tablespoons all-purpose flour
- 300ml beef or vegetable broth
- 1 tablespoon Worcestershire sauce
- 1 cup frozen peas
- Salt and pepper to taste
- Olive oil for cooking

For the Mashed Potatoes:

- 4 large potatoes, peeled and diced
- 50g butter
- 1/2 cup milk
- Salt and pepper to taste

Instructions:

For the Filling:

> In a large skillet, heat olive oil over medium heat. Add chopped onions and cook until softened.
> Add minced garlic and diced carrots to the skillet. Sauté for a few minutes until the carrots start to soften.
> Add the minced lamb or beef to the skillet, breaking it apart with a spoon. Cook until browned.
> Stir in the tomato paste and flour, cooking for an additional 2-3 minutes.
> Pour in the beef or vegetable broth and Worcestershire sauce. Bring the mixture to a simmer, allowing it to thicken. Season with salt and pepper.
> Add frozen peas to the skillet and cook until they are heated through.

Remove the skillet from heat and set aside.

For the Mashed Potatoes:

Boil the peeled and diced potatoes in a pot of salted water until tender.
Drain the potatoes and mash them with butter and milk until smooth. Season with salt and pepper.

Assembling Shepherd's Pie:

Preheat the oven to 200°C (400°F).
Transfer the meat filling to a baking dish, spreading it evenly.
Spoon the mashed potatoes over the top of the meat filling, smoothing the surface with a spatula.
Use a fork to create a decorative pattern on the mashed potato surface.
Bake in the preheated oven for about 20-25 minutes or until the top is golden brown.
Remove from the oven and let it rest for a few minutes before serving.

Shepherd's Pie is a hearty and wholesome dish, perfect for a comforting family meal.

Enjoy its rich flavors and the delightful combination of savory meat and creamy mashed potatoes.

Bangers and Mash

Ingredients:

For the Bangers:

- 8 pork sausages
- 2 tablespoons vegetable oil

For the Mash:

- 6 large potatoes, peeled and cut into chunks
- 1/2 cup milk
- 50g butter
- Salt and pepper to taste

For the Onion Gravy:

- 2 large onions, thinly sliced
- 2 tablespoons vegetable oil
- 2 tablespoons all-purpose flour
- 500ml beef or vegetable broth
- 1 tablespoon Worcestershire sauce
- Salt and pepper to taste

Instructions:

For the Bangers:

Preheat the oven to 200°C (400°F).
Place the sausages on a baking sheet, drizzle with vegetable oil, and bake in the preheated oven for 20-25 minutes or until cooked through and golden brown.

For the Mash:

Boil the peeled and diced potatoes in a large pot of salted water until tender. Drain the potatoes and mash them with butter and milk until smooth. Season with salt and pepper.

For the Onion Gravy:

In a large skillet, heat vegetable oil over medium heat. Add sliced onions and cook until soft and caramelized.
Sprinkle flour over the caramelized onions and stir well to combine.
Gradually pour in the beef or vegetable broth, stirring constantly to avoid lumps.
Add Worcestershire sauce, salt, and pepper. Simmer the gravy until it thickens to your desired consistency.

Assembling Bangers and Mash:

Serve a generous portion of mashed potatoes on each plate.
Place cooked sausages on top of the mashed potatoes.
Pour the onion gravy over the sausages and mashed potatoes.
Garnish with chopped fresh parsley if desired.

Bangers and Mash is a comforting and satisfying dish, showcasing the delicious combination of flavorful sausages, creamy mashed potatoes, and savory onion gravy. Enjoy this classic British and Irish favorite!

Dublin Coddle

Ingredients:

- 8 pork sausages
- 8 slices of bacon, chopped
- 4 large potatoes, peeled and sliced
- 2 onions, thinly sliced
- 2 cloves garlic, minced
- 2 tablespoons fresh parsley, chopped
- Salt and pepper to taste
- 500ml chicken or vegetable broth
- 1 tablespoon vegetable oil

Instructions:

Preheat the oven to 180°C (350°F).
In a large ovenproof casserole dish or Dutch oven, heat the vegetable oil over medium heat.
Add the chopped bacon and cook until it starts to crisp.
Remove the bacon and set it aside. In the same pan, brown the sausages on all sides. Once browned, remove them and set aside.
Add sliced onions to the pan and sauté until they become translucent.
Layer the sliced potatoes on the bottom of the casserole dish.
Place the browned sausages and bacon on top of the potatoes.
Sprinkle minced garlic and chopped fresh parsley over the sausages and bacon.
Season with salt and pepper.
Pour the chicken or vegetable broth over the entire dish.
Cover the casserole dish with a lid or foil and place it in the preheated oven.
Bake for approximately 1.5 to 2 hours or until the potatoes are tender and the sausages are fully cooked.
Check the seasoning and adjust with salt and pepper if needed.
Serve hot, garnished with additional fresh parsley if desired.

Dublin Coddle is often enjoyed with crusty bread or Irish soda bread. It's a delicious and comforting dish, perfect for a cold day or when you're craving a taste of traditional Irish cuisine.

Boxty

Ingredients:

- 2 cups raw potatoes, peeled and grated
- 2 cups mashed potatoes (leftover or freshly mashed)
- 1 cup all-purpose flour
- 1 cup buttermilk
- 1 teaspoon baking soda
- 1/2 teaspoon salt
- Butter or oil for frying

Instructions:

Place the grated raw potatoes in a clean kitchen towel and squeeze out any excess liquid.
In a large mixing bowl, combine the grated raw potatoes, mashed potatoes, flour, baking soda, and salt.
Gradually add buttermilk to the mixture, stirring continuously until you achieve a thick, pancake-like batter. Adjust the consistency with more buttermilk if needed.
Heat a skillet or griddle over medium-high heat and add a little butter or oil.
Spoon the Boxty batter onto the hot skillet, forming small pancakes.
Cook each pancake for 3-4 minutes on each side or until they are golden brown and cooked through.
Repeat the process with the remaining batter, adding more butter or oil to the skillet as needed.
Serve the Boxty pancakes hot, with toppings like sour cream, smoked salmon, or your favorite savory accompaniments.

Boxty is a versatile dish that can be adapted to various preferences. It's a delightful addition to an Irish breakfast or a tasty side dish for lunch or dinner. Enjoy the unique texture and flavor of this traditional Irish treat!

Irish Soda Bread

Ingredients:

- 4 cups all-purpose flour
- 1 teaspoon baking soda (bicarbonate of soda)
- 1 teaspoon salt
- 1 and 3/4 cups buttermilk (or make your own by adding 1 tablespoon of white vinegar or lemon juice to 1 and 3/4 cups milk and let it sit for 5 minutes)

Instructions:

Preheat your oven to 425°F (220°C). Dust a baking sheet with a bit of flour.
In a large mixing bowl, whisk together the all-purpose flour, baking soda, and salt.
Make a well in the center of the dry ingredients and pour in most of the buttermilk.
Using a wooden spoon or your hands, stir the mixture in a circular motion, gradually incorporating the flour from the sides of the bowl. Add more buttermilk as needed until you have a soft, slightly sticky dough.
Turn the dough out onto a floured surface and gently knead it a couple of times to shape it into a round loaf.
Place the dough on the prepared baking sheet. Using a sharp knife, make a deep cross-shaped cut on the top of the loaf. This helps the bread to cook through.
Bake in the preheated oven for about 15 minutes, then reduce the temperature to 400°F (200°C) and continue baking for an additional 20-30 minutes or until the bread is golden brown and sounds hollow when tapped on the bottom.
Allow the Irish Soda Bread to cool on a wire rack before slicing.

Serve the bread with butter and your favorite jams or use it as a side for soups and stews. Irish Soda Bread is best enjoyed on the day it's made, but any leftovers can be toasted for a tasty treat the next day.

Corned Beef and Cabbage

Ingredients:

- 1 corned beef brisket (about 3-4 pounds), with spice packet
- 8 small red potatoes, quartered
- 4 carrots, peeled and cut into chunks
- 1 large head of cabbage, cut into wedges
- 1 onion, peeled and quartered
- 4 cloves garlic, minced
- Water
- Mustard (for serving, optional)

Instructions:

Rinse the corned beef brisket under cold water. Place it in a large pot.
Add the spice packet that came with the corned beef to the pot.
Fill the pot with enough water to cover the brisket. Bring it to a boil over high heat.
Reduce the heat to low, cover the pot, and simmer for about 2 hours or until the meat is tender. Skim off any foam that rises to the surface.
Add the quartered potatoes, carrots, onion, and minced garlic to the pot.
Continue simmering for an additional 30-40 minutes or until the vegetables are tender.
Finally, add the cabbage wedges to the pot and cook for an additional 15-20 minutes or until the cabbage is cooked but still slightly crisp.
Remove the corned beef from the pot and let it rest for a few minutes before slicing it against the grain.
Arrange the sliced corned beef on a platter surrounded by the cooked vegetables.
Serve hot, and optionally, provide mustard on the side for dipping.

Corned Beef and Cabbage is a hearty and flavorful meal that's perfect for a festive St. Patrick's Day celebration or any time you crave a comforting dish with rich, savory flavors.

Guinness Beef Stew

Ingredients:

- 2 pounds stewing beef, cut into bite-sized pieces
- Salt and black pepper to taste
- 1/4 cup all-purpose flour
- 2 tablespoons vegetable oil
- 1 large onion, chopped
- 3 cloves garlic, minced
- 2 tablespoons tomato paste
- 2 tablespoons all-purpose flour
- 1 can (14.9 oz) Guinness stout
- 4 cups beef broth
- 1 tablespoon Worcestershire sauce
- 1 teaspoon sugar
- 1 teaspoon dried thyme
- 2 bay leaves
- 4 large carrots, peeled and cut into chunks
- 4 medium potatoes, peeled and cut into chunks
- Fresh parsley for garnish

Instructions:

Season the stewing beef with salt and black pepper. Dredge the beef pieces in flour, shaking off excess.

In a large Dutch oven or heavy pot, heat the vegetable oil over medium-high heat. Brown the beef in batches until all sides are well-seared. Remove the beef and set aside.

In the same pot, add chopped onions and sauté until they become translucent. Add minced garlic and sauté for an additional 1-2 minutes.

Stir in tomato paste and cook for 2 minutes.

Sprinkle 2 tablespoons of flour over the onion mixture and stir well to combine. Pour in the Guinness stout, scraping the bottom of the pot to release any browned bits.

Return the browned beef to the pot. Add beef broth, Worcestershire sauce, sugar, dried thyme, and bay leaves. Stir well to combine.

Bring the stew to a simmer, then reduce the heat to low. Cover the pot and let it simmer gently for 1.5 to 2 hours or until the beef is tender.

Add carrots and potatoes to the stew. Continue simmering for an additional 30-45 minutes or until the vegetables are cooked.
Adjust seasoning with salt and black pepper as needed.
Remove the bay leaves before serving.
Garnish the Guinness Beef Stew with fresh parsley and serve hot.

Guinness Beef Stew is best enjoyed with a slice of crusty bread to soak up the delicious broth. It's a comforting and satisfying dish, perfect for cold days or when you're in the mood for a classic Irish meal.

Irish Coffee

Ingredients:

- 1 cup hot brewed coffee
- 1 to 1.5 ounces (30 to 45ml) Irish whiskey
- 1 to 2 teaspoons brown sugar (adjust to taste)
- Freshly whipped cream

Instructions:

Brew a cup of your favorite strong coffee.
While the coffee is brewing, warm your favorite Irish coffee mug by rinsing it with hot water.
Pour the hot coffee into the warmed mug, leaving some space at the top.
Add brown sugar to the coffee and stir until it dissolves. Adjust the sweetness according to your taste.
Pour the Irish whiskey into the coffee and stir gently to combine.
In a separate bowl, whip the cream until it's slightly thickened but still pourable.
Hold a spoon over the surface of the coffee and slowly pour the whipped cream over the back of the spoon. This will help the cream float on top of the coffee.
Allow the cream to rest on top, creating a distinct layer.
Do not stir after adding the cream; instead, enjoy the rich combination of hot coffee, whiskey, and cool cream.
Serve immediately and savor the layers of flavor in each sip.

Irish Coffee is a classic and comforting beverage, perfect for chilly evenings or as a delightful conclusion to a meal. Adjust the whiskey and sugar quantities to suit your preferences and enjoy the warmth and flavor of this iconic Irish drink.

Colcannon

Ingredients:

- 4 large potatoes, peeled and cut into chunks
- 1/2 cup unsalted butter (divided)
- 1 cup finely chopped kale or cabbage
- 1 cup scallions (green onions), finely chopped
- 1/2 cup whole milk or heavy cream
- Salt and black pepper to taste

Instructions:

Boil the peeled and chopped potatoes in a large pot of salted water until they are fork-tender.
In a separate pot, melt 1/4 cup of butter over medium heat. Add the chopped kale or cabbage and sauté until wilted and softened.
Drain the boiled potatoes and return them to the pot.
Mash the potatoes with a potato masher or fork until smooth.
Add the sautéed kale or cabbage to the mashed potatoes and mix well.
In a small saucepan, heat the milk or cream and the remaining 1/4 cup of butter until the butter is melted and the mixture is warmed.
Pour the warm milk or cream mixture over the mashed potatoes and kale, stirring continuously.
Add the finely chopped scallions to the mixture, and season with salt and black pepper to taste. Mix until everything is well combined.
Serve the Colcannon hot, with an extra pat of butter on top if desired.

Colcannon is often served alongside boiled ham or bacon, but it can also be enjoyed as a tasty side dish with various meat or vegetarian main courses. It's a classic Irish comfort food, perfect for celebrating St. Patrick's Day or any time you crave a hearty and flavorful side dish.

Irish Lamb Pie

Ingredients:

For the Lamb Stew Filling:

- 2 pounds lamb shoulder or leg, cut into bite-sized pieces
- Salt and black pepper to taste
- 2 tablespoons vegetable oil
- 1 large onion, chopped
- 2 cloves garlic, minced
- 2 carrots, peeled and diced
- 2 celery stalks, diced
- 2 tablespoons all-purpose flour
- 1 tablespoon tomato paste
- 2 cups beef or lamb broth
- 1 cup red wine (optional)
- 1 teaspoon dried thyme
- 1 teaspoon dried rosemary
- 1 cup frozen peas (optional)

For the Pastry Crust:

- 2 1/2 cups all-purpose flour
- 1 cup unsalted butter, cold and cubed
- 1/2 teaspoon salt
- 1/2 cup cold water

Instructions:

For the Lamb Stew Filling:

> Season the lamb pieces with salt and black pepper.
> In a large pot or Dutch oven, heat the vegetable oil over medium-high heat. Brown the lamb pieces in batches until they are well-seared. Remove and set aside.
> In the same pot, add chopped onions and garlic. Sauté until the onions are softened.
> Add diced carrots and celery to the pot and cook for a few minutes until they begin to soften.
> Sprinkle flour over the vegetables and stir well to coat.

Stir in tomato paste and cook for an additional 2 minutes.
Gradually add the beef or lamb broth, stirring constantly to avoid lumps.
Return the seared lamb pieces to the pot. Add red wine, dried thyme, and dried rosemary.
Bring the mixture to a simmer, then reduce the heat to low. Cover and let it simmer for 1.5 to 2 hours or until the lamb is tender.
Add frozen peas in the last 10 minutes of cooking, if desired.

For the Pastry Crust:

In a large mixing bowl, combine the flour and salt.
Add cold, cubed butter to the flour mixture. Use a pastry cutter or your fingers to cut the butter into the flour until the mixture resembles coarse crumbs.
Gradually add cold water to the mixture, stirring with a fork until the dough comes together.
Turn the dough out onto a floured surface and knead it briefly to bring it together.

Assembling the Irish Lamb Pie:

Preheat the oven to 400°F (200°C).
Divide the pastry dough in half. Roll out one half to fit the bottom of a pie dish.
Pour the lamb stew filling into the pie dish.
Roll out the remaining pastry dough and place it on top of the filling. Seal the edges and cut slits in the crust to allow steam to escape.
Bake in the preheated oven for 25-30 minutes or until the crust is golden brown.
Allow the Irish Lamb Pie to cool slightly before serving.

Serve the Irish Lamb Pie with a side of mashed potatoes or your favorite vegetables for a hearty and satisfying meal. Enjoy this comforting Irish classic!

Irish Potato Soup

Ingredients:

- 2 tablespoons unsalted butter
- 1 onion, chopped
- 2 leeks, cleaned and sliced
- 3 cloves garlic, minced
- 4 large potatoes, peeled and diced
- 4 cups chicken or vegetable broth
- Salt and black pepper to taste
- 1 cup whole milk or heavy cream
- Fresh chives or parsley for garnish (optional)

Instructions:

> In a large pot, melt the butter over medium heat.
> Add chopped onions and sliced leeks to the pot. Sauté until the vegetables are softened.
> Add minced garlic and continue to sauté for an additional 1-2 minutes until fragrant.
> Add diced potatoes to the pot and pour in the chicken or vegetable broth. Season with salt and black pepper to taste.
> Bring the mixture to a boil, then reduce the heat to low. Cover the pot and let it simmer for about 15-20 minutes or until the potatoes are tender.
> Use an immersion blender to blend the soup until smooth. Alternatively, transfer the soup in batches to a blender and blend until smooth. Be cautious, as hot liquids can splatter.
> Return the blended soup to the pot. Stir in the whole milk or heavy cream.
> Adjust the seasoning if needed and continue to simmer for an additional 5-10 minutes.
> Serve the Irish Potato Soup hot, garnished with fresh chives or parsley if desired.

This Irish Potato Soup is perfect for a cozy meal, especially during colder months. It can be enjoyed on its own or served with crusty bread for a more substantial meal. Feel free to customize the soup by adding grated cheese, crumbled bacon, or a dollop of sour cream for extra richness.

Irish Cheddar and Ale Soup

Ingredients:

- 4 tablespoons unsalted butter
- 1 large onion, finely chopped
- 2 carrots, peeled and diced
- 2 celery stalks, diced
- 3 cloves garlic, minced
- 1/3 cup all-purpose flour
- 2 cups chicken or vegetable broth
- 2 cups Irish ale (such as Guinness)
- 3 cups whole milk
- 1 bay leaf
- 1 teaspoon dried thyme
- 1 teaspoon Worcestershire sauce
- Salt and black pepper to taste
- 4 cups sharp Irish cheddar cheese, shredded
- 1 tablespoon Dijon mustard
- Fresh chives or parsley for garnish

Instructions:

In a large pot, melt the butter over medium heat.
Add chopped onions, diced carrots, and diced celery to the pot. Sauté until the vegetables are softened.
Add minced garlic and continue to sauté for an additional 1-2 minutes.
Sprinkle flour over the vegetables and stir well to create a roux. Cook for 2-3 minutes to eliminate the raw flour taste.
Gradually whisk in the chicken or vegetable broth, followed by the Irish ale and whole milk. Whisk continuously to avoid lumps.
Add the bay leaf, dried thyme, Worcestershire sauce, salt, and black pepper to the pot. Stir well.
Bring the mixture to a simmer, then reduce the heat to low. Let it simmer for about 15-20 minutes, stirring occasionally, until the soup thickens.
Remove the bay leaf from the soup.
Gradually add the shredded Irish cheddar cheese to the soup, stirring until it's melted and well incorporated.
Stir in the Dijon mustard and continue to simmer for an additional 5-10 minutes.
Adjust the seasoning if needed.

Serve the Irish Cheddar and Ale Soup hot, garnished with fresh chives or parsley.

Enjoy this creamy and flavorful soup with a side of crusty bread or a slice of Irish soda bread. It's a comforting dish that celebrates the rich flavors of Irish cheddar and ale.

Black Pudding

Ingredients:

- 1 liter fresh pig's blood
- 250g oatmeal
- 250g barley or pearl barley
- 1 large onion, finely chopped
- 250g pork fat, finely chopped
- Salt and pepper to taste
- 1 teaspoon dried herbs (thyme, sage, or other herbs of your choice)
- Natural casings (hog casings work well)

Instructions:

Prepare Casings:
- Soak the natural casings in cold water to soften them. Rinse thoroughly and flush water through the casings.

Cook Grains:
- Cook the oatmeal and barley in separate pots according to the package instructions. Drain and let them cool.

Prepare Ingredients:
- In a large mixing bowl, combine the cooked oatmeal, barley, chopped onion, chopped pork fat, and dried herbs. Mix well.

Add Blood:
- Gradually add the fresh pig's blood to the mixture while stirring continuously. Ensure that the blood is well combined with the other ingredients.

Season:
- Season the mixture with salt and pepper to taste. Remember that the blood may need a decent amount of salt to enhance the flavor.

Stuff Casings:
- Using a sausage stuffer or a funnel, fill the natural casings with the blood and grain mixture. Tie the ends of the sausages with kitchen twine.

Cook:
- Bring a large pot of water to a gentle simmer. Place the black pudding sausages in the water and simmer for about 1-2 hours.

Cool and Store:
- Once cooked, let the black pudding sausages cool. They can be stored in the refrigerator for a few days or frozen for longer storage.

Serve:
- Black pudding can be enjoyed by slicing it and either frying or grilling the slices until they are crispy on the outside.

Note: The ingredients and cooking process may vary based on regional traditions and personal preferences. Always check and follow local regulations regarding the use of fresh blood in cooking.

Black pudding is a traditional component of full breakfasts in some cultures and is known for its unique taste and texture. It's often served with other breakfast items like eggs, bacon, and grilled tomatoes.

Dublin Lawyer

Ingredients:

- 2 lobster tails (about 8-10 ounces each), shell-on
- 4 tablespoons unsalted butter
- 2 tablespoons Irish whiskey (such as Jameson)
- 1 cup heavy cream
- Salt and black pepper to taste
- Fresh chives or parsley for garnish (optional)
- Lemon wedges for serving

Instructions:

Prepare Lobster Tails:
- Using kitchen shears, cut the top side of the lobster tails' shells to expose the meat without removing it. Press the shell open slightly to reveal the meat.

Cook Lobster:
- In a large pan or skillet, melt 2 tablespoons of butter over medium-high heat. Place the lobster tails in the pan, meat side down. Cook for 3-4 minutes until the meat begins to brown.

Add Whiskey:
- Pour the Irish whiskey over the lobster tails. Be cautious, as the alcohol may ignite. If it does, allow it to flame for a few seconds until it burns off.

Finish Cooking:
- Flip the lobster tails and cook for an additional 2-3 minutes. Remove the lobster from the pan and set aside.

Prepare Sauce:
- In the same pan, add the remaining 2 tablespoons of butter. Once melted, pour in the heavy cream, stirring to combine. Season with salt and black pepper to taste.

Simmer:
- Allow the cream sauce to simmer and thicken slightly. Adjust the seasoning if needed.

Combine:
- Return the cooked lobster tails to the pan, coating them in the creamy whiskey sauce. Cook for an additional 2 minutes, allowing the lobster to absorb the flavors.

Serve:

- Plate the lobster tails, spooning the sauce over them. Garnish with fresh chives or parsley if desired. Serve with lemon wedges on the side.

Dublin Lawyer is often served over rice or with crusty bread to soak up the delicious sauce. It's a decadent and flavorful dish that showcases the richness of Irish whiskey and the succulence of lobster. Enjoy this special treat for a festive occasion or a luxurious meal.

Irish Apple Cake

Ingredients:

For the Cake:

- 2 cups all-purpose flour
- 1 teaspoon baking powder
- 1/2 teaspoon baking soda
- 1/2 teaspoon ground cinnamon
- 1/4 teaspoon ground nutmeg
- 1/4 teaspoon salt
- 1/2 cup unsalted butter, softened
- 1 cup granulated sugar
- 2 large eggs
- 1 teaspoon vanilla extract
- 1 cup sour cream
- 2 large apples, peeled, cored, and diced (e.g., Granny Smith or Braeburn)

For the Topping:

- 2 tablespoons granulated sugar
- 1/2 teaspoon ground cinnamon

Instructions:

Preheat the Oven:
- Preheat your oven to 350°F (175°C). Grease and flour a 9-inch round cake pan.

Prepare Dry Ingredients:
- In a medium bowl, whisk together the flour, baking powder, baking soda, ground cinnamon, ground nutmeg, and salt. Set aside.

Cream Butter and Sugar:
- In a large mixing bowl, cream together the softened butter and granulated sugar until light and fluffy.

Add Eggs and Vanilla:
- Beat in the eggs one at a time, ensuring each is fully incorporated. Add the vanilla extract and mix well.

Incorporate Dry Ingredients:

- Gradually add the dry ingredients to the wet ingredients, mixing until just combined.

Add Sour Cream:
- Gently fold in the sour cream until the batter is smooth and well mixed.

Fold in Apples:
- Carefully fold in the diced apples, distributing them evenly throughout the batter.

Transfer to Pan:
- Pour the batter into the prepared cake pan, spreading it evenly.

Prepare Topping:
- In a small bowl, mix together the granulated sugar and ground cinnamon for the topping.

Add Topping:
- Sprinkle the cinnamon-sugar mixture evenly over the top of the cake batter.

Bake:
- Bake in the preheated oven for 40-45 minutes or until a toothpick inserted into the center comes out clean.

Cool:
- Allow the cake to cool in the pan for about 10 minutes, then transfer it to a wire rack to cool completely.

Serve:
- Once cooled, you can dust the Irish Apple Cake with powdered sugar or serve it with a dollop of whipped cream.

This Irish Apple Cake is perfect for afternoon tea or as a comforting dessert on any occasion. Enjoy the moist and flavorful bites with the goodness of apples and spices.

Irish Whiskey Trifle

Ingredients:

For the Sponge Cake:

- 1 store-bought sponge cake or homemade sponge cake, cut into cubes

For the Custard:

- 2 cups whole milk
- 1 cup heavy cream
- 6 large egg yolks
- 1/2 cup granulated sugar
- 2 tablespoons cornstarch
- 1 teaspoon vanilla extract

For the Whiskey Soaking Liquid:

- 1/2 cup Irish whiskey (such as Jameson)
- 1-2 tablespoons granulated sugar (adjust to taste)

For Assembly:

- Fresh berries (strawberries, raspberries, blueberries)
- Whipped cream
- Toasted slivered almonds (optional)

Instructions:

1. Prepare the Custard:

> In a medium saucepan, heat the whole milk and heavy cream over medium heat until it just begins to simmer. Do not let it boil.
> In a separate bowl, whisk together the egg yolks, granulated sugar, and cornstarch until well combined.
> Gradually whisk the hot milk mixture into the egg yolk mixture, tempering the eggs.
> Return the combined mixture to the saucepan and cook over medium heat, stirring constantly, until the custard thickens. It should coat the back of a spoon.
> Remove the custard from heat and stir in the vanilla extract. Let it cool.

2. Prepare the Whiskey Soaking Liquid:

In a small bowl, mix the Irish whiskey with 1-2 tablespoons of granulated sugar, adjusting the sweetness to your taste.

3. Assemble the Trifle:

   Arrange half of the sponge cake cubes in the bottom of a trifle dish.
   Drizzle half of the whiskey soaking liquid over the sponge cake.
   Spoon half of the cooled custard over the sponge cake layer.
   Add a layer of fresh berries.
   Repeat the layers with the remaining sponge cake, whiskey soaking liquid, custard, and berries.
   Finish with a layer of whipped cream on top.
   Optionally, sprinkle toasted slivered almonds over the whipped cream.
   Refrigerate the trifle for at least 4 hours or overnight to allow the flavors to meld.
   Serve chilled and enjoy the rich and flavorful layers of this Irish Whiskey Trifle.

This Irish Whiskey Trifle is a show-stopping dessert that combines the sweetness of the custard and berries with the warmth of Irish whiskey. It's a perfect treat for festive occasions or special celebrations.

Irish Boxty Pancakes

Ingredients:

- 1 cup raw potatoes, peeled and grated
- 1 cup cooked mashed potatoes
- 1 cup all-purpose flour
- 1 teaspoon baking powder
- 1 teaspoon salt
- 1 cup buttermilk
- 1 large egg
- Butter or oil for cooking

Instructions:

Prepare Raw Potatoes:
- Peel and grate the raw potatoes. Place the grated potatoes in a clean kitchen towel and squeeze out excess moisture.

Mix Ingredients:
- In a mixing bowl, combine the grated raw potatoes, cooked mashed potatoes, flour, baking powder, and salt.

Add Buttermilk and Egg:
- In a separate bowl, whisk together the buttermilk and egg. Add this mixture to the potato and flour mixture, stirring until well combined. The consistency should be like a thick pancake batter.

Cooking:
- Heat a griddle or non-stick skillet over medium heat. Add a little butter or oil to coat the surface.

Scoop Batter:
- Drop spoonfuls of the batter onto the hot griddle to form pancakes. Use the back of the spoon to spread the batter into a round shape.

Cook Until Golden:
- Cook the pancakes for 3-4 minutes on each side, or until they are golden brown and cooked through.

Serve Warm:
- Serve the Boxty Pancakes warm. They can be enjoyed on their own or with toppings like sour cream, applesauce, or smoked salmon.

Optional: Keep Warm in Oven:
- If making a larger batch, you can keep the cooked pancakes warm in a low-temperature oven until ready to serve.

Irish Boxty Pancakes are a versatile dish that can be served for breakfast, brunch, or as a side dish with savory toppings. They have a rustic and hearty texture with the comforting flavors of potatoes. Enjoy this traditional Irish treat!

Colcannon Soup

Ingredients:

- 2 tablespoons unsalted butter
- 1 onion, finely chopped
- 2 leeks, cleaned and sliced
- 3 cloves garlic, minced
- 4 cups potatoes, peeled and diced
- 4 cups green cabbage, finely shredded
- 6 cups chicken or vegetable broth
- Salt and black pepper to taste
- 1 cup milk or cream
- Chopped fresh parsley for garnish

Instructions:

Sauté Vegetables:
- In a large pot, melt the butter over medium heat. Add the chopped onion and sliced leeks. Sauté until the vegetables are softened.

Add Garlic and Potatoes:
- Add minced garlic to the pot and sauté for an additional 1-2 minutes. Add the diced potatoes and cook for another 5 minutes, stirring occasionally.

Add Cabbage:
- Stir in the finely shredded cabbage and cook for another 5 minutes until the cabbage begins to wilt.

Pour Broth:
- Pour in the chicken or vegetable broth. Season with salt and black pepper to taste. Bring the mixture to a boil, then reduce the heat to low. Cover and simmer for about 15-20 minutes or until the potatoes are tender.

Blend or Mash:
- Use an immersion blender to partially blend the soup, leaving some chunks for texture. Alternatively, you can use a potato masher to mash some of the potatoes and cabbage.

Add Milk or Cream:
- Pour in the milk or cream, stirring to combine. Adjust the seasoning if needed. Simmer for an additional 5-10 minutes.

Serve:
- Ladle the Colcannon Soup into bowls. Garnish with chopped fresh parsley.

Optional: Serve with Crispy Bacon:

- For an extra layer of flavor, you can top each serving with crispy bacon pieces.

Colcannon Soup is a hearty and flavorful dish that brings together the classic Irish flavors of potatoes and cabbage in a comforting soup form. It's perfect for warming up on a cold day or as a delicious addition to your St. Patrick's Day menu.

Beef and Guinness Pie

Ingredients:

For the Filling:

- 2 pounds stewing beef, cubed
- 2 tablespoons all-purpose flour
- Salt and black pepper to taste
- 2 tablespoons vegetable oil
- 2 onions, chopped
- 2 cloves garlic, minced
- 2 carrots, sliced
- 2 celery stalks, sliced
- 1 can (14 ounces) Guinness beer
- 2 cups beef broth
- 2 tablespoons tomato paste
- 2 tablespoons Worcestershire sauce
- 2 teaspoons dried thyme
- 2 bay leaves

For the Pastry:

- 2 sheets of store-bought puff pastry, thawed
- 1 egg, beaten (for egg wash)

Instructions:

Preparing the Filling:

> Preheat the oven to 350°F (175°C).
> In a bowl, toss the cubed beef with flour, salt, and black pepper until the beef is coated.
> In a large, ovenproof pot, heat the vegetable oil over medium-high heat. Add the beef in batches and brown on all sides. Remove the beef and set it aside.
> In the same pot, add the chopped onions, minced garlic, sliced carrots, and sliced celery. Sauté until the vegetables are softened.
> Return the browned beef to the pot. Pour in the Guinness beer, beef broth, and add tomato paste, Worcestershire sauce, dried thyme, and bay leaves. Stir to combine.

Bring the mixture to a simmer, then cover the pot and transfer it to the preheated oven. Bake for about 2 hours or until the beef is tender and the flavors have melded.

Assembling the Pie:

Once the filling is ready, remove the bay leaves and discard them.
Roll out one sheet of puff pastry and line the bottom of a pie dish. Trim any excess pastry.
Pour the beef and Guinness filling into the pie dish.
Roll out the second sheet of puff pastry and use it to cover the filling. Seal the edges and cut a few slits in the top to allow steam to escape.
Brush the top of the pastry with beaten egg for a golden finish.
Bake in the oven at 375°F (190°C) for 25-30 minutes or until the pastry is golden and puffed.
Allow the Beef and Guinness Pie to cool for a few minutes before serving.

This Beef and Guinness Pie is a savory and satisfying dish that pairs well with mashed potatoes or a side of green vegetables. It's a great choice for a comforting meal, especially during colder seasons or for St. Patrick's Day celebrations.

Irish Seafood Chowder

Ingredients:

- 1 pound mixed seafood (such as cod, salmon, shrimp, mussels, or scallops), cleaned and chopped if necessary
- 2 tablespoons olive oil
- 1 onion, finely chopped
- 2 leeks, cleaned and sliced
- 2 carrots, diced
- 2 celery stalks, diced
- 2 cloves garlic, minced
- 3 tablespoons all-purpose flour
- 4 cups fish or vegetable broth
- 1 cup potatoes, peeled and diced
- 1 bay leaf
- 1 teaspoon dried thyme
- Salt and black pepper to taste
- 1 cup whole milk or heavy cream
- Chopped fresh parsley for garnish
- Crusty bread for serving

Instructions:

Prepare Seafood:
- If needed, clean and chop the seafood into bite-sized pieces.

Sauté Vegetables:
- In a large pot, heat the olive oil over medium heat. Add the chopped onion, sliced leeks, diced carrots, diced celery, and minced garlic. Sauté until the vegetables are softened.

Add Flour:
- Sprinkle the flour over the sautéed vegetables and stir well to coat them. Cook for 1-2 minutes to remove the raw taste of the flour.

Pour Broth:
- Gradually pour in the fish or vegetable broth, stirring continuously to avoid lumps. Bring the mixture to a simmer.

Add Potatoes and Herbs:
- Add the diced potatoes, bay leaf, dried thyme, salt, and black pepper to the pot. Simmer until the potatoes are tender.

Add Seafood:

- Gently add the mixed seafood to the pot and simmer until the seafood is cooked through. This usually takes only a few minutes, as seafood cooks quickly.

Stir in Milk or Cream:
- Pour in the whole milk or heavy cream, stirring to combine. Allow the chowder to heat through without boiling.

Adjust Seasoning:
- Taste the chowder and adjust the seasoning if needed. Remove the bay leaf.

Serve:
- Ladle the Irish Seafood Chowder into bowls. Garnish with chopped fresh parsley and serve with crusty bread.

Irish Seafood Chowder is a comforting and satisfying dish, perfect for seafood lovers. It's a great way to enjoy the flavors of the ocean in a warm and creamy soup, especially during cooler seasons. Serve it as a main course or as a delightful starter for a special meal.

Beef and Mushroom Boxty

Ingredients:

For the Boxty Pancakes:

- 2 cups raw potatoes, peeled and grated
- 1 cup cooked mashed potatoes
- 1 cup all-purpose flour
- 1 teaspoon baking powder
- Salt and black pepper to taste
- 1 cup buttermilk
- 1 large egg
- Butter or oil for cooking

For the Beef and Mushroom Filling:

- 1 pound beef stew meat, cubed
- 2 tablespoons all-purpose flour
- Salt and black pepper to taste
- 2 tablespoons vegetable oil
- 1 onion, finely chopped
- 2 cloves garlic, minced
- 8 ounces mushrooms, sliced
- 1 cup beef broth
- 1 cup Guinness beer
- 2 tablespoons tomato paste
- 1 tablespoon Worcestershire sauce
- 1 teaspoon dried thyme
- Chopped fresh parsley for garnish

Instructions:

For the Boxty Pancakes:

In a bowl, combine the grated raw potatoes, cooked mashed potatoes, flour, baking powder, salt, and black pepper.
In a separate bowl, whisk together the buttermilk and egg.
Gradually add the wet ingredients to the potato mixture, stirring until well combined. The consistency should be like a thick pancake batter.
Heat a griddle or non-stick skillet over medium heat. Add a little butter or oil to coat the surface.

Drop spoonfuls of the batter onto the hot griddle to form pancakes. Use the back of the spoon to spread the batter into a round shape.

Cook the pancakes for 3-4 minutes on each side, or until they are golden brown and cooked through. Set the boxty pancakes aside.

For the Beef and Mushroom Filling:

In a bowl, toss the cubed beef with flour, salt, and black pepper until the beef is coated.

In a large, ovenproof pot, heat the vegetable oil over medium-high heat. Add the beef in batches and brown on all sides. Remove the beef and set it aside.

In the same pot, add the chopped onion, minced garlic, and sliced mushrooms. Sauté until the vegetables are softened.

Return the browned beef to the pot. Pour in the beef broth, Guinness beer, and add tomato paste, Worcestershire sauce, and dried thyme. Stir to combine.

Bring the mixture to a simmer, then cover the pot and transfer it to the preheated oven. Bake for about 2 hours or until the beef is tender and the flavors have melded.

Assembling the Beef and Mushroom Boxty:

Once the filling is ready, place a spoonful of the beef and mushroom mixture onto each boxty pancake.

Fold or roll the boxty pancakes around the filling.

Garnish with chopped fresh parsley.

Serve the Beef and Mushroom Boxty warm, and enjoy the hearty combination of tender beef, savory mushrooms, and traditional Irish boxty pancakes.

Irish Bacon and Cabbage

Ingredients:

- 1.5 to 2 pounds Irish back bacon or loin (rashers or a joint)
- 1 small to medium-sized cabbage, cut into wedges
- 6 to 8 medium-sized potatoes, peeled and quartered
- Salt and black pepper, to taste
- Optional: Butter for serving

Instructions:

- Prepare the Bacon:
    - If using a joint of bacon, place it in a large pot and cover it with water. Bring the water to a boil and then reduce the heat to a simmer. Allow the bacon to simmer for about 30 minutes per pound, or until cooked through.
- Add Potatoes:
    - Once the bacon is almost cooked, add the quartered potatoes to the pot. Continue simmering until the potatoes are tender.
- Add Cabbage:
    - About 15-20 minutes before the end of cooking, add the cabbage wedges to the pot. This will allow the cabbage to cook until tender but not overcooked.
- Check Doneness:
    - Pierce the potatoes with a fork to check for tenderness. Ensure the bacon is fully cooked by checking its internal temperature (it should reach at least 145°F or 63°C).
- Serve:
    - Once everything is cooked, carefully remove the bacon joint from the pot and let it rest for a few minutes before slicing. Arrange the sliced bacon, boiled potatoes, and cabbage wedges on a serving platter.
- Season and Serve:
    - Season with salt and black pepper to taste. If desired, serve with a pat of butter on top of the boiled potatoes.
- Optional: Parsley Sauce or Mustard:
    - Some variations include serving the dish with parsley sauce or mustard on the side for added flavor.
- Enjoy:
    - Serve the Irish Bacon and Cabbage hot, family-style, and enjoy this comforting and traditional Irish meal.

Irish Bacon and Cabbage is a straightforward and hearty dish that brings together the flavors of bacon, cabbage, and potatoes. It's a wonderful way to celebrate Irish cuisine and is often associated with festive occasions, particularly St. Patrick's Day.

Traditional Irish Breakfast

Ingredients:

- Irish Pork Sausages:
  - 4-6 traditional Irish pork sausages
- Irish Rashers (Bacon):
  - 8 slices of Irish bacon (rashers)
- Black Pudding:
  - 4 slices of black pudding
- White Pudding:
  - 4 slices of white pudding
- Irish Eggs:
  - 4 eggs
- Tomatoes:
  - 2 large tomatoes, halved
- Mushrooms:
  - 8-10 button mushrooms, sliced
- Irish Soda Bread or Toast:
  - 4 slices of Irish soda bread or toast
- Butter:
  - For frying and spreading on bread
- Salt and Black Pepper:
  - To taste

Instructions:

Cook the Sausages:
- In a large frying pan, cook the Irish sausages until browned and cooked through. Set aside.

Cook the Rashers (Bacon):
- In the same pan, fry the Irish bacon rashers until crispy. Set aside with the sausages.

Cook the Black and White Pudding:
- Fry the slices of black and white pudding in the pan until heated through and crispy on the outside. Set aside with the sausages and bacon.

Prepare the Tomatoes and Mushrooms:
- In the same pan, cook the halved tomatoes and sliced mushrooms until softened.

Fry the Eggs:

- Fry the eggs to your liking in the same pan. You can cook them sunny-side-up, over-easy, or poached.

Toast the Bread:
- Toast slices of Irish soda bread or regular toast.

Assemble the Breakfast:
- Arrange the cooked sausages, rashers, black pudding, white pudding, eggs, tomatoes, and mushrooms on a plate. Place the toast or Irish soda bread on the side.

Serve:
- Serve the Traditional Irish Breakfast hot, with butter for the bread, and season with salt and black pepper according to taste.

Optional Additions:
- Some variations may include additional items such as baked beans, hash browns, or grilled potatoes.

The Traditional Irish Breakfast is a substantial and satisfying meal that is often enjoyed on weekends or special occasions. It reflects the hearty and wholesome nature of Irish cuisine and is a delicious way to start the day.

Dubliner Cheese Dip

Ingredients:

- 8 ounces Dubliner cheese, grated
- 4 ounces cream cheese, softened
- 1/2 cup mayonnaise
- 1 clove garlic, minced
- 1 tablespoon Dijon mustard
- 1 tablespoon Worcestershire sauce
- 1 tablespoon fresh chives, chopped (for garnish)
- Salt and black pepper to taste

Instructions:

Grate Dubliner Cheese:
- Grate the Dubliner cheese using a box grater. Set aside.

Prepare Cream Cheese Mixture:
- In a mixing bowl, combine the softened cream cheese, mayonnaise, minced garlic, Dijon mustard, and Worcestershire sauce. Mix until smooth and well combined.

Add Grated Dubliner Cheese:
- Fold in the grated Dubliner cheese into the cream cheese mixture. Ensure that the cheese is evenly distributed.

Season the Dip:
- Season the dip with salt and black pepper to taste. Keep in mind that Dubliner cheese has a naturally salty flavor, so adjust accordingly.

Chill the Dip:
- Cover the bowl with plastic wrap and refrigerate the dip for at least 1-2 hours. Chilling allows the flavors to meld and enhances the texture.

Garnish and Serve:
- Before serving, garnish the Dubliner Cheese Dip with chopped fresh chives. This adds a pop of color and freshness.

Serve with Accompaniments:
- Serve the Dubliner Cheese Dip with an assortment of accompaniments such as crackers, sliced baguette, pretzels, or vegetable sticks.

Enjoy:
- Enjoy the creamy and flavorful Dubliner Cheese Dip as a delicious appetizer or party snack.

This dip showcases the unique taste of Dubliner cheese, which combines the characteristics of cheddar, Swiss, and Parmesan. It's a delightful addition to any gathering, and its rich and nutty flavor pairs well with various dippers.

Irish Chicken Pot Pie

Ingredients:

For the Filling:

- 1.5 pounds boneless, skinless chicken breasts or thighs, cooked and shredded
- 2 tablespoons olive oil
- 1 onion, finely chopped
- 2 carrots, diced
- 2 celery stalks, diced
- 1 cup frozen peas
- 1 cup frozen corn
- 1/3 cup all-purpose flour
- 4 cups chicken broth
- 1 cup whole milk or heavy cream
- 2 teaspoons dried thyme
- Salt and black pepper to taste

For the Pastry Crust:

- 2 sheets of store-bought puff pastry, thawed
- 1 egg, beaten (for egg wash)

Instructions:

For the Filling:

Cook and Shred Chicken:
- Cook the chicken until fully cooked, either by baking, boiling, or using leftover cooked chicken. Shred the cooked chicken into bite-sized pieces.

Sauté Vegetables:
- In a large pot, heat olive oil over medium heat. Add chopped onion, diced carrots, and diced celery. Sauté until the vegetables are softened.

Make Roux:
- Sprinkle the flour over the sautéed vegetables and stir to create a roux. Cook for 1-2 minutes to remove the raw taste of the flour.

Add Broth and Milk:
- Gradually add the chicken broth and whole milk (or heavy cream), stirring continuously to avoid lumps. Bring the mixture to a simmer.

Thicken and Season:

- Once the mixture has thickened, add the shredded chicken, frozen peas, frozen corn, dried thyme, salt, and black pepper. Stir to combine. Simmer for a few more minutes until the vegetables are heated through.

Prepare Pastry Crust:
- While the filling is simmering, preheat the oven to the temperature specified on the puff pastry package. Roll out the puff pastry sheets on a floured surface to fit the size of your baking dish.

Assembling the Chicken Pot Pie:

Transfer Filling to Baking Dish:
- Pour the chicken and vegetable filling into a greased baking dish.

Top with Puff Pastry:
- Place the rolled-out puff pastry over the filling in the baking dish, covering it completely. Trim any excess pastry.

Seal Edges and Brush with Egg Wash:
- Press the edges of the pastry to seal them to the dish. Brush the top of the puff pastry with beaten egg for a golden finish.

Bake:
- Bake in the preheated oven according to the puff pastry package instructions or until the crust is golden brown and flaky.

Serve:
- Allow the Irish Chicken Pot Pie to cool for a few minutes before serving. Slice and enjoy the delicious combination of creamy chicken filling and crispy puff pastry.

Irish Chicken Pot Pie is a comforting and crowd-pleasing dish, perfect for family dinners or special occasions. The creamy filling and flaky pastry make it a delightful and satisfying meal.

Whiskey Glazed Salmon

Ingredients:

For the Whiskey Glaze:

- 1/4 cup whiskey (Irish whiskey or your choice)
- 1/4 cup brown sugar, packed
- 2 tablespoons soy sauce
- 1 tablespoon Dijon mustard
- 1 tablespoon honey
- 2 cloves garlic, minced
- 1 teaspoon grated fresh ginger
- 1/2 teaspoon black pepper

For the Salmon:

- 4 salmon fillets
- Salt and black pepper to taste
- 2 tablespoons olive oil
- Optional: Chopped fresh parsley for garnish
- Lemon wedges for serving

Instructions:

For the Whiskey Glaze:

Prepare the Glaze:
- In a small saucepan, combine whiskey, brown sugar, soy sauce, Dijon mustard, honey, minced garlic, grated ginger, and black pepper.

Simmer and Reduce:
- Bring the mixture to a simmer over medium heat. Allow it to simmer for about 5-7 minutes or until the glaze has thickened slightly. Stir occasionally to prevent sticking.

Set Aside:
- Once the glaze has reached a syrupy consistency, remove it from the heat and set it aside.

For the Salmon:

Prepare the Salmon:
- Pat the salmon fillets dry with paper towels. Season both sides of the fillets with salt and black pepper.

Pan-Sear the Salmon:
- In a large skillet, heat olive oil over medium-high heat. Place the salmon fillets in the skillet, skin side down if they have skin. Sear for about 3-4 minutes on each side, or until the salmon is golden brown and cooked to your liking.

Brush with Glaze:
- In the last minute of cooking, brush the whiskey glaze over the salmon fillets, ensuring they are well coated. Allow the glaze to caramelize slightly.

Garnish and Serve:
- Remove the salmon from the skillet, place it on a serving platter, and brush with additional glaze if desired. Garnish with chopped fresh parsley.

Serve with Lemon Wedges:
- Serve the Whiskey Glazed Salmon hot, with lemon wedges on the side for a burst of citrus flavor.

This Whiskey Glazed Salmon is a sophisticated yet easy-to-make dish that's perfect for a special dinner. The combination of sweet, savory, and smoky flavors enhances the natural taste of the salmon, creating a memorable dining experience.

Irish Nachos

Ingredients:

For the Potato Slices:

- 4 large russet potatoes, scrubbed and sliced into thin rounds
- 2 tablespoons olive oil
- 1 teaspoon garlic powder
- 1 teaspoon paprika
- Salt and black pepper to taste

For the Toppings:

- 1 cup shredded cheddar cheese
- 1/2 cup cooked and crumbled bacon
- 1/4 cup sliced green onions
- 1/4 cup chopped fresh parsley or cilantro
- Sour cream for serving

Optional Additions:

- Sliced jalapeños
- Diced tomatoes
- Guacamole

Instructions:

Preheat the Oven:
- Preheat your oven to 425°F (220°C).

Prepare the Potato Slices:
- In a large bowl, toss the potato slices with olive oil, garlic powder, paprika, salt, and black pepper until evenly coated.

Arrange on Baking Sheet:
- Arrange the seasoned potato slices in a single layer on a baking sheet lined with parchment paper.

Bake the Potato Slices:
- Bake in the preheated oven for about 20-25 minutes or until the potato slices are golden and crispy, flipping them halfway through the baking time.

Assemble the Nachos:

- Once the potato slices are crispy, remove them from the oven and transfer them to a serving platter or a large plate.

Add Toppings:
- Sprinkle shredded cheddar cheese over the hot potato slices, allowing the heat to melt the cheese. Add cooked and crumbled bacon, sliced green onions, and chopped fresh parsley or cilantro on top.

Optional: Add More Toppings:
- If desired, add additional toppings such as sliced jalapeños, diced tomatoes, or a dollop of guacamole.

Serve with Sour Cream:
- Serve the Irish Nachos hot, with a side of sour cream for dipping.

Irish Nachos are a crowd-pleasing and flavorful snack that brings together the best elements of loaded nachos with a uniquely Irish twist. The crispy potato slices provide a hearty base for the tasty toppings, making it a delicious and satisfying treat for any occasion.

Potato Leek Soup

Ingredients:

- 3 tablespoons unsalted butter
- 3 leeks, white and light green parts, cleaned and thinly sliced
- 3 large potatoes, peeled and diced
- 4 cups vegetable or chicken broth
- 1 bay leaf
- 1 teaspoon thyme leaves (fresh or dried)
- Salt and black pepper to taste
- 1 cup whole milk or heavy cream (optional, for creamier soup)
- Chopped fresh chives or parsley for garnish

Instructions:

Prepare Leeks:
- Clean the leeks thoroughly as they can be sandy. Slice the leeks thinly, discarding the tough green tops.

Cook Leeks in Butter:
- In a large pot, melt the butter over medium heat. Add the sliced leeks and cook until they are softened, about 5-7 minutes.

Add Potatoes:
- Add the diced potatoes to the pot and stir well with the leeks.

Pour in Broth:
- Pour in the vegetable or chicken broth, ensuring that the leeks and potatoes are fully submerged. Add the bay leaf and thyme leaves.

Simmer:
- Bring the soup to a boil, then reduce the heat to a simmer. Cover the pot and let it simmer for about 15-20 minutes or until the potatoes are tender.

Season:
- Season the soup with salt and black pepper to taste. Remove the bay leaf.

Blend or Mash:
- At this point, you can either use an immersion blender to blend the soup until smooth, or use a potato masher for a chunkier texture.

Add Cream (Optional):
- If you prefer a creamier soup, stir in the whole milk or heavy cream. Adjust the consistency to your liking by adding more broth if needed.

Adjust Seasoning:

- Taste and adjust the seasoning as necessary. Add more salt and pepper if desired.

Serve:
- Ladle the Potato Leek Soup into bowls. Garnish with chopped fresh chives or parsley.

Enjoy:
- Serve the Potato Leek Soup hot, and enjoy this simple and flavorful comfort dish.

Potato Leek Soup is versatile and can be enjoyed as a light meal or a starter. Its creamy texture and the mild sweetness of leeks make it a comforting choice, especially during colder months.

Irish Cream Cheesecake

Ingredients:

For the Crust:

- 1 1/2 cups graham cracker crumbs
- 1/4 cup granulated sugar
- 1/2 cup unsalted butter, melted

For the Cheesecake Filling:

- 24 ounces (3 packages) cream cheese, softened
- 1 cup granulated sugar
- 4 large eggs
- 1 cup Irish cream liqueur (e.g., Baileys)
- 1 teaspoon vanilla extract
- 1/4 cup all-purpose flour

For the Topping (Optional):

- Whipped cream
- Chocolate shavings or cocoa powder

Instructions:

For the Crust:

> Preheat the Oven:
> - Preheat your oven to 325°F (163°C). Grease a 9-inch springform pan.
>
> Mix Crust Ingredients:
> - In a bowl, combine graham cracker crumbs, sugar, and melted butter. Press the mixture firmly into the bottom of the prepared springform pan to form the crust.
>
> Bake the Crust:
> - Bake the crust in the preheated oven for 10 minutes. Remove from the oven and let it cool while you prepare the cheesecake filling.

For the Cheesecake Filling:

> Prepare Cream Cheese Mixture:
> - In a large mixing bowl, beat the softened cream cheese until smooth and creamy.
>
> Add Sugar and Eggs:

- Add the granulated sugar and beat until well combined. Add the eggs one at a time, beating well after each addition.

Incorporate Irish Cream and Vanilla:
- Pour in the Irish cream liqueur and vanilla extract. Mix until smooth and creamy.

Fold in Flour:
- Gently fold in the flour until just combined. Be careful not to overmix.

Pour into Crust:
- Pour the cream cheese mixture over the prepared crust in the springform pan.

Bake the Cheesecake:
- Bake the cheesecake in the preheated oven for approximately 60-70 minutes, or until the center is set and the top is lightly golden.

Cool and Refrigerate:
- Allow the cheesecake to cool in the oven with the door ajar for about an hour. Then, refrigerate for at least 4 hours or overnight.

For the Topping (Optional):

Whipped Cream and Chocolate:
- Before serving, you can add a layer of whipped cream on top and sprinkle with chocolate shavings or cocoa powder for an extra touch of indulgence.

Slice and Serve:
- Slice the Irish Cream Cheesecake and serve chilled. Enjoy the rich and flavorful dessert!

Irish Cream Cheesecake is a delightful treat that combines the smoothness of cheesecake with the luxurious taste of Irish cream. It's perfect for special occasions or as a decadent ending to a festive meal.

Steak and Guinness Pie

Ingredients:

For the Filling:

- 2 pounds (about 1 kg) stewing beef, cut into bite-sized pieces
- Salt and black pepper to taste
- 3 tablespoons all-purpose flour
- 3 tablespoons vegetable oil
- 2 onions, chopped
- 3 cloves garlic, minced
- 2 carrots, peeled and diced
- 2 celery stalks, diced
- 1 cup mushrooms, sliced
- 1 can (14.9 oz) Guinness stout
- 2 cups beef broth
- 2 tablespoons tomato paste
- 2 teaspoons Worcestershire sauce
- 1 teaspoon dried thyme
- 2 bay leaves

For the Pastry:

- 2 sheets of store-bought puff pastry, thawed
- 1 egg, beaten (for egg wash)

Instructions:

For the Filling:

Preheat the Oven:
- Preheat your oven to 375°F (190°C).

Season and Coat Beef:
- Season the stewing beef with salt and black pepper. Coat the beef pieces in flour, shaking off any excess.

Brown the Beef:
- In a large ovenproof pot, heat vegetable oil over medium-high heat. Brown the beef in batches until well-seared on all sides. Remove the beef and set it aside.

Sauté Vegetables:
- In the same pot, add chopped onions, minced garlic, diced carrots, diced celery, and sliced mushrooms. Sauté until the vegetables are softened.

Deglaze with Guinness:
- Pour in the Guinness stout to deglaze the pot, scraping the flavorful bits from the bottom.

Add Remaining Filling Ingredients:
- Return the browned beef to the pot. Add beef broth, tomato paste, Worcestershire sauce, dried thyme, and bay leaves. Stir well to combine.

Simmer:
- Bring the mixture to a simmer. Cover the pot and transfer it to the preheated oven. Allow it to cook for about 2 hours or until the beef is tender.

Check and Adjust Seasoning:
- Taste the filling and adjust the seasoning if necessary. Remove and discard the bay leaves.

For the Pastry:

Prepare the Pastry:
- Roll out the puff pastry sheets on a floured surface to fit the size of your baking dish.

Assemble the Pie:
- Pour the beef and vegetable filling into a greased baking dish. Place the rolled-out puff pastry over the filling, covering it completely. Trim any excess pastry.

Seal Edges and Brush with Egg Wash:
- Press the edges of the pastry to seal them to the dish. Brush the top of the puff pastry with beaten egg for a golden finish.

Bake:
- Bake in the preheated oven for about 25-30 minutes or until the pastry is golden brown and puffed.

Serve:
- Allow the Steak and Guinness Pie to cool for a few minutes before serving. Slice and enjoy this comforting and savory dish.

Steak and Guinness Pie is a classic comfort food, perfect for warming up on chilly days. The combination of tender beef, vegetables, and rich Guinness creates a flavorful filling, while the flaky puff pastry adds a delicious finishing touch.

Irish Lamb Stew

Ingredients:

- 2 pounds boneless lamb stew meat, cut into cubes
- 2 tablespoons vegetable oil
- 2 tablespoons all-purpose flour
- Salt and black pepper to taste
- 2 large onions, chopped
- 2 cloves garlic, minced
- 4 cups beef or lamb broth
- 1 cup Guinness stout
- 4 large carrots, peeled and sliced
- 4 medium potatoes, peeled and diced
- 2 tablespoons tomato paste
- 1 tablespoon Worcestershire sauce
- 2 bay leaves
- 1 teaspoon dried thyme
- Chopped fresh parsley for garnish

Instructions:

Prepare the Lamb:
- In a large bowl, toss the lamb cubes with flour, salt, and black pepper until the meat is coated.

Brown the Lamb:
- In a large, heavy pot or Dutch oven, heat vegetable oil over medium-high heat. Brown the lamb cubes on all sides, working in batches to avoid overcrowding. Remove the browned lamb and set it aside.

Sauté Onions and Garlic:
- In the same pot, add chopped onions and minced garlic. Sauté until the onions are softened and translucent.

Deglaze with Guinness:
- Pour in the Guinness stout, scraping the bottom of the pot to loosen any browned bits. Allow it to simmer for a couple of minutes.

Add Remaining Ingredients:
- Return the browned lamb to the pot. Add beef or lamb broth, sliced carrots, diced potatoes, tomato paste, Worcestershire sauce, bay leaves, and dried thyme. Stir well to combine.

Simmer:

- Bring the stew to a boil, then reduce the heat to low. Cover and let it simmer for 1.5 to 2 hours or until the lamb is tender and the flavors meld together.

Adjust Seasoning:
- Taste the stew and adjust the seasoning with salt and pepper if needed. Remove the bay leaves.

Serve:
- Ladle the Irish Lamb Stew into bowls. Garnish with chopped fresh parsley.

Enjoy:
- Serve the stew hot and enjoy the comforting flavors of this traditional Irish dish.

Irish Lamb Stew is often served with crusty bread or Irish soda bread to soak up the delicious broth. It's a wonderful dish for family gatherings and celebrations, providing a taste of Ireland's rich culinary tradition.

Irish Coffee Chocolate Mousse

Ingredients:

- 6 ounces dark chocolate, finely chopped
- 1/4 cup strong brewed coffee, cooled
- 3 tablespoons Irish cream liqueur (e.g., Baileys)
- 3 large eggs, separated
- 2 tablespoons granulated sugar
- 1 cup heavy cream
- Whipped cream and chocolate shavings for garnish (optional)

Instructions:

Melt the Chocolate:
- In a heatproof bowl set over a pot of simmering water (double boiler), melt the finely chopped dark chocolate. Stir until smooth and then remove from heat. Allow it to cool slightly.

Add Coffee and Irish Cream:
- Stir in the strong brewed coffee and Irish cream liqueur into the melted chocolate. Mix until well combined. Let the mixture cool to room temperature.

Whip the Egg Yolks:
- In a separate bowl, whisk the egg yolks until pale and slightly thickened. Gradually add the cooled chocolate mixture to the egg yolks, whisking continuously to avoid scrambling the eggs.

Whip the Egg Whites:
- In another clean, dry bowl, whip the egg whites until soft peaks form. Gradually add the granulated sugar and continue whipping until glossy and stiff peaks form.

Fold in Egg Whites:
- Gently fold the whipped egg whites into the chocolate mixture until no white streaks remain. Be careful not to deflate the egg whites.

Whip the Heavy Cream:
- In a separate bowl, whip the heavy cream until stiff peaks form.

Combine with Chocolate Mixture:
- Fold the whipped cream into the chocolate mixture until well combined. This will create a light and airy mousse.

Chill:

- Spoon the Irish Coffee Chocolate Mousse into serving glasses or bowls. Chill in the refrigerator for at least 4 hours or overnight to allow the mousse to set.

Garnish (Optional):
- Before serving, garnish the mousse with a dollop of whipped cream and chocolate shavings if desired.

Enjoy:
- Serve the Irish Coffee Chocolate Mousse chilled and savor the delightful combination of chocolate, coffee, and Irish cream.

This decadent dessert is perfect for special occasions or as a delightful treat for chocolate and coffee lovers. The addition of Irish cream adds a touch of elegance and a hint of Irish flavor to the classic chocolate mousse.

Dubliner Cheese and Bacon Dip

Ingredients:

- 8 ounces Dubliner cheese, shredded
- 8 ounces cream cheese, softened
- 1 cup sour cream
- 1 cup mayonnaise
- 1 cup cooked bacon, crumbled
- 2 green onions, thinly sliced
- 1 teaspoon Worcestershire sauce
- 1/2 teaspoon garlic powder
- Salt and black pepper to taste
- Fresh chives for garnish (optional)
- Assorted crackers, bread, or vegetables for serving

Instructions:

Preheat the Oven:
- Preheat your oven to 375°F (190°C).

Combine Cheeses:
- In a large mixing bowl, combine the shredded Dubliner cheese and softened cream cheese. Mix until well combined.

Add Sour Cream and Mayonnaise:
- Add sour cream and mayonnaise to the cheese mixture. Mix thoroughly until smooth and creamy.

Fold in Bacon and Green Onions:
- Fold in the crumbled bacon and thinly sliced green onions into the cheese mixture. Reserve a small amount of bacon and green onions for garnish if desired.

Season with Worcestershire, Garlic Powder, Salt, and Pepper:
- Season the dip with Worcestershire sauce, garlic powder, salt, and black pepper. Adjust the seasoning to taste.

Transfer to Baking Dish:
- Transfer the cheese and bacon mixture to a baking dish, spreading it evenly.

Bake:
- Bake in the preheated oven for approximately 20-25 minutes or until the dip is hot and bubbly.

Garnish and Serve:

- Remove the dip from the oven and garnish with the reserved bacon and green onions. Optionally, sprinkle with fresh chives.

Serve Warm:
- Serve the Dubliner Cheese and Bacon Dip warm with assorted crackers, slices of bread, or vegetable sticks.

Enjoy:
- Enjoy this delicious and savory dip with the delightful combination of Dubliner cheese and bacon.

This Dubliner Cheese and Bacon Dip is sure to be a hit at any party or gathering. The creamy texture, smoky bacon, and rich Dubliner cheese create a dip that's both comforting and full of flavor.

Irish Smoked Salmon Boxty

Ingredients:

For the Boxty Pancakes:

- 2 cups raw potatoes, peeled and grated
- 1 cup cooked mashed potatoes
- 1 cup all-purpose flour
- 1 cup buttermilk
- 1 egg
- 1 teaspoon baking soda
- Salt and black pepper to taste
- Butter or oil for cooking

For the Topping:

- Irish smoked salmon slices
- Cream cheese or crème fraîche
- Fresh dill, chopped
- Capers (optional)
- Lemon wedges

Instructions:

For the Boxty Pancakes:

Prepare Raw Potatoes:
- Place the grated raw potatoes in a clean kitchen towel and squeeze out excess moisture.

Combine Ingredients:
- In a large mixing bowl, combine the grated raw potatoes, mashed potatoes, all-purpose flour, buttermilk, egg, baking soda, salt, and black pepper. Mix well to form a batter.

Cook the Boxty Pancakes:
- Heat a skillet or griddle over medium heat and add butter or oil. Spoon the batter onto the hot surface, forming small pancakes. Cook until golden brown on both sides, flipping as needed.

Keep Warm:
- Keep the cooked boxty pancakes warm in a low oven while you prepare the toppings.

Assemble the Irish Smoked Salmon Boxty:

- Top with Cream Cheese or Crème Fraîche:
    - Place a spoonful of cream cheese or crème fraîche on each boxty pancake.
- Add Smoked Salmon:
    - Top the cream cheese with slices of Irish smoked salmon.
- Garnish:
    - Sprinkle chopped fresh dill over the smoked salmon. Add capers if desired.
- Serve with Lemon Wedges:
    - Serve the Irish Smoked Salmon Boxty with lemon wedges on the side.
- Enjoy:
    - Enjoy this delicious and elegant dish with the delightful combination of boxty pancakes and smoked salmon.

Irish Smoked Salmon Boxty makes for a wonderful appetizer or brunch dish. The soft and fluffy boxty pancakes complement the smoky richness of the salmon, while the cream cheese, dill, and capers add layers of flavor. It's a perfect dish for celebrating Irish flavors.

Irish Cream Bread Pudding

Ingredients:

- 6 cups bread cubes (day-old bread works well)
- 1/2 cup raisins or sultanas
- 4 large eggs
- 1 cup granulated sugar
- 2 cups whole milk
- 1 cup heavy cream
- 1/2 cup Irish cream liqueur (e.g., Baileys)
- 1 teaspoon vanilla extract
- 1/2 teaspoon ground cinnamon
- 1/4 teaspoon ground nutmeg
- Pinch of salt
- Butter for greasing the baking dish

For the Irish Cream Sauce:

- 1/2 cup unsalted butter
- 1/2 cup granulated sugar
- 1/2 cup Irish cream liqueur

Instructions:

For the Bread Pudding:

Preheat the Oven:
- Preheat your oven to 350°F (175°C). Grease a baking dish with butter.

Prepare Bread Cubes:
- Cut the bread into cubes, and place them in the prepared baking dish. Sprinkle raisins or sultanas over the bread cubes.

Whisk Eggs and Sugar:
- In a bowl, whisk together eggs and granulated sugar until well combined.

Combine Wet Ingredients:
- In a separate bowl, combine whole milk, heavy cream, Irish cream liqueur, vanilla extract, ground cinnamon, ground nutmeg, and a pinch of salt.

Mix Wet and Dry Ingredients:
- Slowly pour the wet ingredients into the egg and sugar mixture, stirring continuously to avoid curdling.

Pour Over Bread Cubes:
- Pour the combined mixture over the bread cubes and raisins. Gently press down on the bread cubes to ensure they are soaked in the liquid.

Let Soak:
- Allow the bread cubes to soak in the liquid for about 15-20 minutes.

Bake:
- Bake in the preheated oven for 45-50 minutes or until the top is golden brown and the custard is set.

For the Irish Cream Sauce:

Prepare the Sauce:
- In a saucepan, melt butter over medium heat. Add sugar and Irish cream liqueur. Stir continuously until the sugar is dissolved, and the sauce has thickened slightly.

Serve:
- Pour the warm Irish Cream Sauce over the bread pudding just before serving.

Enjoy:
- Serve the Irish Cream Bread Pudding warm, and enjoy the luscious combination of creamy bread pudding with the indulgent Irish cream sauce.

This Irish Cream Bread Pudding is a delightful treat for special occasions or as a comforting dessert. The Irish cream adds a unique and delicious twist to the classic bread pudding, making it a favorite among those who appreciate rich and flavorful desserts.

Irish Whiskey Cake

Ingredients:

For the Cake:

- 1 cup unsalted butter, softened
- 1 cup granulated sugar
- 4 large eggs
- 2 cups all-purpose flour
- 1 teaspoon baking powder
- 1/2 teaspoon baking soda
- 1/4 teaspoon salt
- 1 cup buttermilk
- 1/2 cup Irish whiskey
- 1 teaspoon vanilla extract
- Zest of 1 lemon (optional)
- Zest of 1 orange (optional)

For the Whiskey Soaking Syrup:

- 1/4 cup granulated sugar
- 1/4 cup water
- 1/4 cup Irish whiskey

For the Glaze (Optional):

- 1 cup powdered sugar
- 2-3 tablespoons Irish whiskey

Instructions:

For the Cake:

Preheat the Oven:
- Preheat your oven to 325°F (163°C). Grease and flour a bundt cake pan.

Cream Butter and Sugar:
- In a large mixing bowl, cream together the softened butter and granulated sugar until light and fluffy.

Add Eggs:
- Add the eggs one at a time, beating well after each addition.

Combine Dry Ingredients:

- In a separate bowl, whisk together the flour, baking powder, baking soda, and salt.

Alternate Mixing:
- Gradually add the dry ingredients to the butter and sugar mixture, alternating with buttermilk. Begin and end with the dry ingredients.

Add Whiskey, Vanilla, and Citrus Zest:
- Stir in the Irish whiskey, vanilla extract, and citrus zest (if using). Mix until well combined.

Pour into Pan:
- Pour the batter into the prepared bundt cake pan, spreading it evenly.

Bake:
- Bake in the preheated oven for about 60-70 minutes or until a toothpick inserted into the center comes out clean.

For the Whiskey Soaking Syrup:

Prepare Syrup:
- In a small saucepan, combine sugar, water, and Irish whiskey. Heat over medium heat until the sugar dissolves.

Soak the Cake:
- Once the cake is baked, poke several holes in the top using a toothpick or skewer. Pour the whiskey soaking syrup over the warm cake, allowing it to absorb.

Cool:
- Let the cake cool completely in the pan before removing.

For the Glaze (Optional):

Prepare Glaze:
- In a bowl, whisk together powdered sugar and Irish whiskey until smooth.

Drizzle Over Cake:
- Drizzle the glaze over the cooled cake.

Serve:
- Slice and serve the Irish Whiskey Cake. Enjoy the rich and moist texture with a hint of Irish whiskey flavor.

This Irish Whiskey Cake is a delightful treat that captures the essence of Irish hospitality. The whiskey soaking syrup adds moisture and a distinctive flavor, making it a perfect dessert for celebrating special occasions or simply indulging in a delicious slice of cake.

Dubliner Cheese and Onion Tart

Ingredients:

For the Tart Crust:

- 1 1/4 cups all-purpose flour
- 1/2 cup unsalted butter, cold and diced
- 1/4 teaspoon salt
- 3-4 tablespoons ice water

For the Filling:

- 2 tablespoons olive oil
- 2 large onions, thinly sliced
- 1 teaspoon sugar
- 1 1/2 cups grated Dubliner cheese
- 3 large eggs
- 1 cup heavy cream
- Salt and black pepper to taste
- Fresh thyme leaves for garnish (optional)

Instructions:

For the Tart Crust:

Prepare Tart Crust:
- In a food processor, combine the flour, cold diced butter, and salt. Pulse until the mixture resembles coarse crumbs.

Add Ice Water:
- Add ice water, one tablespoon at a time, and pulse until the dough comes together. Be cautious not to overmix.

Form Dough:
- Turn the dough out onto a floured surface and knead it briefly until it forms a smooth ball. Flatten the dough into a disk, wrap it in plastic wrap, and refrigerate for at least 30 minutes.

Roll Out the Dough:
- Preheat the oven to 375°F (190°C). On a floured surface, roll out the chilled dough into a circle large enough to fit your tart pan. Press the dough into the pan, trimming any excess.

Pre-Bake the Crust:

- Line the tart crust with parchment paper and fill it with pie weights or dried beans. Bake for about 15 minutes. Remove the parchment paper and weights, then bake for an additional 5 minutes until the crust is lightly golden. Set aside to cool.

For the Filling:

Caramelize Onions:
- In a skillet, heat olive oil over medium-low heat. Add thinly sliced onions and cook, stirring occasionally, until they become golden brown and caramelized. Sprinkle sugar over the onions to help with caramelization.

Prepare Filling:
- In a bowl, whisk together eggs, heavy cream, grated Dubliner cheese, salt, and black pepper. Add the caramelized onions and mix well.

Assemble and Bake:
- Pour the filling into the pre-baked tart crust. Bake in the preheated oven for 25-30 minutes or until the filling is set and the top is golden brown.

Garnish:
- If desired, garnish the Dubliner Cheese and Onion Tart with fresh thyme leaves.

Cool and Serve:
- Allow the tart to cool slightly before slicing. Serve warm or at room temperature.

This Dubliner Cheese and Onion Tart is a delightful dish that can be served as a main course or as part of a brunch or appetizer spread. The combination of Dubliner cheese and caramelized onions creates a savory and indulgent flavor profile that's sure to please your taste buds.

Irish Stout Ice Cream

Ingredients:

- 2 cups heavy cream
- 1 cup whole milk
- 3/4 cup granulated sugar
- 1/2 cup Irish stout beer (such as Guinness)
- 1 teaspoon pure vanilla extract
- 4 large egg yolks
- Pinch of salt
- Optional: chocolate chunks or chocolate shavings for added texture

Instructions:

Prepare Ice Cream Base:
- In a medium saucepan, combine the heavy cream, whole milk, and half of the sugar. Heat the mixture over medium heat until it begins to simmer. Stir occasionally to dissolve the sugar.

Whisk Egg Yolks:
- In a separate bowl, whisk together the egg yolks and the remaining sugar until the mixture becomes pale and slightly thickened.

Temper Eggs:
- Slowly pour a small amount of the hot cream mixture into the egg yolks, whisking constantly to temper the eggs. Gradually add more hot cream while whisking.

Combine Mixtures:
- Pour the egg and cream mixture back into the saucepan with the remaining hot cream. Cook over medium heat, stirring constantly with a wooden spoon, until the mixture thickens and coats the back of the spoon. Do not let it boil.

Add Stout and Vanilla:
- Remove the saucepan from heat and stir in the Irish stout beer and vanilla extract. Mix until well combined.

Strain the Mixture:
- Strain the ice cream base through a fine-mesh sieve into a clean bowl to remove any cooked egg bits. Discard any solids.

Cool the Mixture:
- Allow the ice cream base to cool to room temperature. Once cooled, cover the bowl with plastic wrap, pressing it directly onto the surface of the

mixture to prevent a skin from forming. Refrigerate for at least 4 hours or
　　　overnight.
- Churn the Ice Cream:
  - Pour the chilled mixture into an ice cream maker and churn according to the manufacturer's instructions.
- Add Chocolate (Optional):
  - If desired, add chocolate chunks or chocolate shavings during the last few minutes of churning.
- Transfer and Freeze:
  - Transfer the churned ice cream to a lidded container. Freeze for at least 4 hours or until the ice cream reaches the desired firmness.
- Serve and Enjoy:
  - Scoop the Irish Stout Ice Cream into bowls or cones. Garnish with additional chocolate if desired and enjoy the rich and creamy flavors.

This Irish Stout Ice Cream is a delightful treat for those who appreciate the deep, malty notes of Irish stout. It's perfect for serving on its own or alongside a warm dessert like chocolate cake or brownies.

Potato and Leek Boxty

Ingredients:

- 2 cups peeled and grated potatoes
- 1 cup finely chopped leeks (white and light green parts)
- 1 cup all-purpose flour
- 1 teaspoon baking powder
- 1 teaspoon salt
- 1/2 teaspoon black pepper
- 1 cup buttermilk
- 1 large egg
- Butter or oil for cooking

Instructions:

Prepare Potatoes:
- Peel and grate the potatoes using a box grater. Place the grated potatoes in a clean kitchen towel and squeeze out excess moisture.

Combine Ingredients:
- In a large mixing bowl, combine the grated potatoes, chopped leeks, all-purpose flour, baking powder, salt, and black pepper.

Mix Wet Ingredients:
- In a separate bowl, whisk together the buttermilk and egg.

Combine Wet and Dry Ingredients:
- Pour the wet ingredients into the potato and leek mixture. Stir until well combined. The consistency should be similar to pancake batter.

Preheat Griddle or Pan:
- Preheat a griddle or non-stick skillet over medium heat. Add a bit of butter or oil to coat the surface.

Cook Boxty Pancakes:
- Spoon the batter onto the hot griddle, forming small pancakes. Cook for 3-4 minutes on each side or until golden brown and cooked through.

Keep Warm:
- Keep the cooked Potato and Leek Boxty warm in a low oven while you cook the remaining pancakes.

Serve:
- Serve the boxty pancakes warm as a side dish or with your favorite toppings, such as sour cream or applesauce.

Enjoy:

- Enjoy the delicious combination of grated potatoes and leeks in this traditional Irish dish!

Potato and Leek Boxty is a versatile dish that can be enjoyed for breakfast, brunch, or as a side dish for a savory meal. The leeks add a mild onion flavor, while the grated potatoes provide a hearty and satisfying texture. Serve them with your favorite toppings or alongside other Irish dishes for a complete meal.

Baileys Irish Cream Cheesecake

Ingredients:

For the Crust:

- 1 1/2 cups graham cracker crumbs
- 1/4 cup granulated sugar
- 1/2 cup unsalted butter, melted

For the Cheesecake Filling:

- 24 ounces (about 680g) cream cheese, softened
- 1 cup granulated sugar
- 3 large eggs
- 1 cup sour cream
- 1/2 cup Baileys Irish Cream
- 1 teaspoon vanilla extract
- 2 tablespoons all-purpose flour

For the Baileys Ganache (Optional):

- 1/2 cup semi-sweet chocolate chips
- 1/4 cup heavy cream
- 2 tablespoons Baileys Irish Cream

Instructions:

For the Crust:

Preheat Oven:
- Preheat your oven to 325°F (163°C).

Prepare Crust:
- In a bowl, combine graham cracker crumbs, sugar, and melted butter. Press the mixture into the bottom of a 9-inch (23cm) springform pan to form the crust.

Bake Crust:
- Bake the crust in the preheated oven for about 10 minutes. Remove from the oven and let it cool while you prepare the filling.

For the Cheesecake Filling:

Prepare Cream Cheese Mixture:
- In a large mixing bowl, beat the softened cream cheese until smooth.

Add Sugar:
- Add the sugar and continue to beat until well combined.

Add Eggs:
- Add the eggs one at a time, beating well after each addition.

Incorporate Sour Cream, Baileys, and Vanilla:
- Mix in the sour cream, Baileys Irish Cream, and vanilla extract until smooth.

Add Flour:
- Gradually add the flour and mix until just combined. Be careful not to overmix.

Pour Over Crust:
- Pour the cream cheese mixture over the prepared crust in the springform pan.

Bake:
- Bake in the preheated oven for about 55-60 minutes or until the center is set and the top is lightly browned.

Cool:
- Allow the cheesecake to cool in the oven with the door ajar for about an hour. Then, refrigerate for at least 4 hours or overnight.

For the Baileys Ganache (Optional):

Prepare Ganache:
- In a small saucepan, heat the heavy cream until it just begins to simmer. Remove from heat and stir in the chocolate chips until smooth. Add Baileys Irish Cream and mix until well combined.

Pour Over Cheesecake:
- Pour the Baileys ganache over the chilled cheesecake, spreading it evenly.

Chill:
- Place the cheesecake back in the refrigerator for the ganache to set.

Serve:
- Once the ganache is set, remove the cheesecake from the springform pan, slice, and serve.

Baileys Irish Cream Cheesecake is a decadent dessert that's perfect for special occasions or as a treat for Baileys lovers. The combination of the creamy cheesecake filling and the Baileys-infused ganache creates a delicious and indulgent flavor profile. Enjoy a slice of this delightful cheesecake with a cup of coffee or as a sweet ending to a festive meal.

Dubliner Cheese and Herb Scones

Ingredients:

- 2 cups all-purpose flour
- 2 teaspoons baking powder
- 1/2 teaspoon baking soda
- 1/2 teaspoon salt
- 1/2 cup unsalted butter, cold and diced
- 1 cup Dubliner cheese, grated
- 1 tablespoon fresh parsley, chopped
- 1 teaspoon fresh thyme leaves
- 1/2 teaspoon dried rosemary, crushed
- 1 cup buttermilk
- 1 tablespoon Dijon mustard (optional, for added flavor)
- Extra grated Dubliner cheese for topping

Instructions:

Preheat Oven:
- Preheat your oven to 425°F (220°C). Line a baking sheet with parchment paper.

Prepare Dry Ingredients:
- In a large mixing bowl, whisk together the flour, baking powder, baking soda, and salt.

Incorporate Butter:
- Add the cold diced butter to the dry ingredients. Use a pastry cutter or your fingertips to rub the butter into the flour until the mixture resembles coarse crumbs.

Add Cheese and Herbs:
- Stir in the grated Dubliner cheese, chopped parsley, thyme leaves, and crushed rosemary.

Combine Wet Ingredients:
- In a separate bowl, whisk together the buttermilk and Dijon mustard (if using).

Mix Wet and Dry Ingredients:
- Pour the wet ingredients into the dry ingredients. Mix until just combined. Be careful not to overmix.

Shape the Dough:

- Turn the dough out onto a floured surface and gently knead it a few times until it comes together. Pat the dough into a circle about 1 inch (2.5 cm) thick.

Cut Scones:
- Use a round cutter to cut out scones from the dough. Place the scones on the prepared baking sheet, leaving some space between them.

Top with Cheese:
- Sprinkle extra grated Dubliner cheese on top of each scone.

Bake:
- Bake in the preheated oven for 12-15 minutes or until the scones are golden brown and cooked through.

Cool:
- Allow the scones to cool on a wire rack for a few minutes.

Serve:
- Serve the Dubliner Cheese and Herb Scones warm, either on their own or with a pat of butter.

These scones are perfect for serving as a side with soups, salads, or on their own as a tasty snack. The Dubliner cheese adds a rich and nutty flavor, while the blend of herbs provides a delightful aromatic quality. Enjoy these scones fresh from the oven for a delightful treat.

Irish Whiskey Truffles

Ingredients:

- 8 ounces (about 227g) dark chocolate, finely chopped
- 1/2 cup (120ml) heavy cream
- 2 tablespoons unsalted butter
- 2 tablespoons Irish whiskey
- Cocoa powder or melted chocolate for coating (optional)

Instructions:

Prepare Chocolate:
- Place the finely chopped dark chocolate in a heatproof bowl.

Heat Cream:
- In a small saucepan, heat the heavy cream over medium heat until it just begins to simmer. Do not boil.

Pour Over Chocolate:
- Pour the hot cream over the chopped chocolate. Let it sit for a minute to soften the chocolate.

Stir:
- Gently stir the chocolate and cream until smooth and well combined. If needed, you can place the bowl over a pot of simmering water (double boiler) to melt any remaining chocolate.

Add Butter and Whiskey:
- Stir in the unsalted butter until completely melted. Then, add the Irish whiskey and mix until smooth and glossy.

Chill:
- Cover the bowl with plastic wrap and refrigerate the mixture for at least 2 hours or until firm.

Shape Truffles:
- Once the mixture has chilled and set, use a spoon or melon baller to scoop out portions and shape them into small truffle-sized balls. Place the shaped truffles on a parchment-lined tray.

Optional Coating:
- If desired, you can roll the truffles in cocoa powder or dip them in melted chocolate for a glossy finish. This step is optional but adds extra flavor and a professional touch.

Chill Again:

- Place the coated truffles back in the refrigerator for about 30 minutes to set.

Serve:
- Once the Irish Whiskey Truffles are fully set, transfer them to a serving plate or box. They are now ready to be enjoyed!

These Irish Whiskey Truffles make a delightful homemade gift or a special treat for yourself. The combination of dark chocolate and Irish whiskey creates a luxurious and indulgent flavor that's perfect for dessert or as an after-dinner treat. Store the truffles in the refrigerator until you're ready to enjoy them.

Irish Potato Boxty

Ingredients:

- 2 large potatoes, peeled and grated
- 1 cup mashed potatoes (leftover or freshly mashed)
- 1 cup all-purpose flour
- 1 teaspoon baking powder
- 1 teaspoon salt
- 1/2 teaspoon black pepper
- 1 cup buttermilk
- 1 large egg
- Butter or oil for cooking

Instructions:

Grate Potatoes:
- Peel and grate the two large potatoes using a box grater. Place the grated potatoes in a clean kitchen towel and squeeze out excess moisture.

Combine Ingredients:
- In a large mixing bowl, combine the grated potatoes, mashed potatoes, all-purpose flour, baking powder, salt, and black pepper.

Add Buttermilk and Egg:
- In a separate bowl, whisk together the buttermilk and egg. Pour this mixture into the potato mixture and stir until well combined. The consistency should be similar to pancake batter.

Preheat Griddle or Pan:
- Preheat a griddle or non-stick skillet over medium heat. Add a bit of butter or oil to coat the surface.

Cook Boxty Pancakes:
- Spoon the batter onto the hot griddle, forming small pancakes. Cook for 3-4 minutes on each side or until golden brown and cooked through.

Keep Warm:
- Keep the cooked Irish Potato Boxty warm in a low oven while you cook the remaining pancakes.

Serve:
- Serve the boxty pancakes warm as a side dish or with your favorite toppings, such as sour cream or applesauce.

Enjoy:
- Enjoy the unique and comforting flavors of Irish Potato Boxty!

Irish Potato Boxty is a versatile dish that pairs well with various toppings or can be enjoyed on its own. Whether served for breakfast, brunch, or as a side dish with savory accompaniments, this traditional Irish pancake is sure to be a delightful addition to your meals.

Irish Cream Chocolate Tart

Ingredients:

For the Tart Shell:

- 1 1/2 cups all-purpose flour
- 1/2 cup unsweetened cocoa powder
- 1/2 cup powdered sugar
- 1/4 teaspoon salt
- 1 cup cold unsalted butter, cut into small pieces
- 1 large egg yolk
- 2 tablespoons ice water

For the Chocolate Filling:

- 8 ounces (about 227g) dark chocolate, finely chopped
- 1 cup heavy cream
- 1/4 cup unsalted butter
- 1/4 cup Irish cream liqueur
- 1 teaspoon vanilla extract

Instructions:

For the Tart Shell:

> Prepare Tart Dough:
> - In a food processor, combine the flour, cocoa powder, powdered sugar, and salt. Pulse to mix.
>
> Add Butter:
> - Add the cold butter pieces and pulse until the mixture resembles coarse crumbs.
>
> Add Egg Yolk and Water:
> - In a small bowl, whisk together the egg yolk and ice water. Add this mixture to the food processor and pulse until the dough starts to come together.
>
> Form Dough:
> - Turn the dough out onto a lightly floured surface and knead it a few times to bring it together. Form it into a disk, wrap in plastic wrap, and refrigerate for at least 30 minutes.
>
> Roll Out and Line Tart Pan:
> - Preheat your oven to 375°F (190°C). On a floured surface, roll out the chilled dough to fit a tart pan. Press the dough into the pan, trim any excess, and prick the bottom with a fork.

Pre-Bake:
- Line the tart shell with parchment paper and fill it with pie weights or dried beans. Bake for about 15 minutes. Remove the weights and parchment, then bake for an additional 5-7 minutes or until the crust is set. Allow it to cool completely.

For the Chocolate Filling:

Prepare Chocolate:
- Place the finely chopped dark chocolate in a heatproof bowl.

Heat Cream and Butter:
- In a saucepan, heat the heavy cream and butter over medium heat until it just begins to simmer. Pour the hot cream and butter over the chopped chocolate.

Mix Until Smooth:
- Let it sit for a minute to soften the chocolate, then stir until the mixture is smooth and glossy.

Add Irish Cream and Vanilla:
- Stir in the Irish cream liqueur and vanilla extract until well combined.

Fill the Tart Shell:
- Pour the chocolate filling into the cooled tart shell, spreading it evenly.

Chill:
- Place the tart in the refrigerator to chill and set for at least 2 hours or until firm.

Serve:
- Once set, slice and serve the Irish Cream Chocolate Tart. Optionally, garnish with whipped cream or a dusting of cocoa powder.

This Irish Cream Chocolate Tart is a luxurious and decadent dessert that's perfect for special occasions or as a delightful treat for chocolate lovers. The combination of the velvety chocolate filling and the hint of Irish cream creates a flavor profile that's both sophisticated and indulgent.

Dubliner Cheese and Bacon Scones

Ingredients:

- 2 cups all-purpose flour
- 1 tablespoon baking powder
- 1/2 teaspoon salt
- 1/2 cup unsalted butter, cold and diced
- 1 cup Dubliner cheese, grated
- 4 slices bacon, cooked and crumbled
- 1/2 cup green onions, finely chopped
- 3/4 cup buttermilk
- 1 large egg, beaten (for egg wash)

Instructions:

Preheat Oven:
- Preheat your oven to 425°F (220°C). Line a baking sheet with parchment paper.

Prepare Dry Ingredients:
- In a large mixing bowl, whisk together the flour, baking powder, and salt.

Add Butter:
- Add the cold diced butter to the dry ingredients. Use a pastry cutter or your fingertips to rub the butter into the flour until the mixture resembles coarse crumbs.

Incorporate Cheese, Bacon, and Green Onions:
- Stir in the grated Dubliner cheese, crumbled bacon, and chopped green onions.

Add Buttermilk:
- Pour in the buttermilk and stir until the dough just comes together. Be careful not to overmix.

Knead Dough:
- Turn the dough out onto a floured surface and gently knead it a few times until it comes together.

Shape and Cut Scones:
- Pat the dough into a circle about 1 inch (2.5 cm) thick. Use a round cutter to cut out scones from the dough. Place the scones on the prepared baking sheet.

Brush with Egg Wash:

- Brush the tops of the scones with the beaten egg to give them a golden finish.

Bake:
- Bake in the preheated oven for 12-15 minutes or until the scones are golden brown and cooked through.

Cool:
- Allow the Dubliner Cheese and Bacon Scones to cool on a wire rack for a few minutes.

Serve:
- Serve the scones warm, either on their own or with a pat of butter.

These savory scones are perfect for brunch, as a side with soups or salads, or as a delicious snack. The combination of Dubliner cheese, bacon, and green onions creates a flavor explosion that's sure to be a hit. Enjoy these scones fresh from the oven for the best taste and texture.

Irish Cream Tiramisu

Ingredients:

For the Coffee Soaking Liquid:

- 1 cup strong brewed coffee, cooled
- 2 tablespoons Irish cream liqueur (e.g., Baileys)

For the Tiramisu Filling:

- 4 large egg yolks
- 3/4 cup granulated sugar
- 1 cup mascarpone cheese, softened
- 1 1/2 cups heavy cream
- 1 teaspoon vanilla extract
- 3 tablespoons Irish cream liqueur

For Assembling the Tiramisu:

- Ladyfinger cookies (about 24)
- Unsweetened cocoa powder, for dusting
- Chocolate shavings or grated chocolate (optional, for garnish)

Instructions:

1. Coffee Soaking Liquid:

    In a shallow dish, combine the brewed coffee and Irish cream liqueur. Set aside.

2. Tiramisu Filling:

    In a heatproof bowl, whisk together the egg yolks and granulated sugar. Place the bowl over a pot of simmering water (double boiler) and whisk continuously until the mixture becomes pale and slightly thickened. Remove from heat.
    Add the softened mascarpone cheese to the egg yolk mixture and whisk until smooth.
    In a separate bowl, whip the heavy cream until stiff peaks form. Fold the whipped cream into the mascarpone mixture until well combined.
    Add vanilla extract and Irish cream liqueur, gently folding until the filling is smooth and creamy.

3. Assembling the Tiramisu:

Quickly dip each ladyfinger into the coffee and Irish cream mixture, ensuring they are coated but not overly soaked.

Arrange a layer of soaked ladyfingers in the bottom of a serving dish or individual glasses.

Spread half of the mascarpone filling over the layer of ladyfingers, smoothing it out with a spatula.

Repeat the process with another layer of soaked ladyfingers and the remaining mascarpone filling.

Cover and refrigerate the Irish Cream Tiramisu for at least 4 hours or preferably overnight to allow the flavors to meld.

4. Serving:

Before serving, dust the top of the Tiramisu with unsweetened cocoa powder.

Optionally, garnish with chocolate shavings or grated chocolate for an extra touch.

Serve chilled and enjoy the rich and creamy Irish Cream Tiramisu!

This Irish Cream Tiramisu is a delightful dessert with a twist, perfect for special occasions or to indulge in a bit of luxury. The combination of coffee, Irish cream, and the luscious mascarpone filling creates a decadent and satisfying treat.

Whiskey Glazed Chicken Wings

Ingredients:

For the Chicken Wings:

- 2 pounds chicken wings, split at joints, tips discarded
- Salt and pepper, to taste
- 1 teaspoon garlic powder
- 1 teaspoon onion powder
- 1 teaspoon paprika
- 1 tablespoon vegetable oil

For the Whiskey Glaze:

- 1/2 cup whiskey (choose your favorite type)
- 1/4 cup soy sauce
- 1/4 cup honey
- 2 tablespoons brown sugar
- 2 cloves garlic, minced
- 1 teaspoon grated fresh ginger
- 1 tablespoon cornstarch (optional, for thickening)

Instructions:

1. Preheat the Oven:

    Preheat your oven to 400°F (200°C).

2. Season the Chicken Wings:

    In a large bowl, season the chicken wings with salt, pepper, garlic powder, onion powder, and paprika.
    Add vegetable oil and toss the wings until evenly coated.

3. Bake the Chicken Wings:

    Place the seasoned chicken wings on a baking sheet lined with parchment paper.
    Bake in the preheated oven for about 40-45 minutes or until the wings are golden brown and crispy.

4. Prepare the Whiskey Glaze:

In a saucepan, combine whiskey, soy sauce, honey, brown sugar, minced garlic, and grated ginger.

Bring the mixture to a simmer over medium heat, stirring occasionally.

Optional: If you prefer a thicker glaze, mix cornstarch with a small amount of water to create a slurry. Add the slurry to the simmering sauce and stir until thickened.

5. Glaze the Chicken Wings:

Once the chicken wings are cooked, transfer them to a large bowl.

Pour the whiskey glaze over the wings and toss until they are thoroughly coated.

6. Serve:

Arrange the glazed chicken wings on a serving platter.

Optionally, garnish with sesame seeds, chopped green onions, or cilantro for added freshness.

Serve the whiskey glazed chicken wings hot and enjoy!

These wings are perfect for game day, parties, or any occasion where you want to impress your guests with a tasty and slightly boozy treat. The combination of the crispy wings and the sweet and savory whiskey glaze is sure to be a crowd-pleaser.

Irish Coffee Panna Cotta

Ingredients:

For the Panna Cotta:

- 2 cups heavy cream
- 1/2 cup whole milk
- 1/2 cup granulated sugar
- 2 teaspoons instant coffee granules or espresso powder
- 3 teaspoons unflavored gelatin
- 1/4 cup cold water
- 2 tablespoons Irish whiskey (e.g., Jameson)

For the Coffee Sauce:

- 1/2 cup strong brewed coffee
- 2 tablespoons Irish whiskey
- 2 tablespoons maple syrup or honey

Instructions:

For the Panna Cotta:

In a small bowl, sprinkle the gelatin over cold water and let it sit for 5-10 minutes to bloom.

In a saucepan, heat the heavy cream, whole milk, sugar, and instant coffee over medium heat. Stir until the sugar and coffee are fully dissolved, and the mixture is hot but not boiling.

Remove the saucepan from heat and stir in the bloomed gelatin until completely dissolved.

Let the mixture cool for a few minutes, then stir in the Irish whiskey.

Strain the mixture through a fine-mesh sieve into a pouring jug or individual serving glasses to remove any undissolved coffee granules.

Pour the Panna Cotta mixture into serving glasses or ramekins.

Refrigerate for at least 4 hours or until set.

For the Coffee Sauce:

In a small saucepan, combine the strong brewed coffee, Irish whiskey, and maple syrup (or honey).

Simmer over low heat for about 5-7 minutes, stirring occasionally, until the sauce thickens slightly.

Let the coffee sauce cool to room temperature.

Serving:

Once the Panna Cotta is set, spoon a generous drizzle of the coffee sauce over each serving.
Optionally, garnish with a sprinkle of cocoa powder or chocolate shavings.
Serve chilled and enjoy the luxurious Irish Coffee Panna Cotta!

This dessert is a delightful way to end a meal, combining the classic flavors of Irish coffee with the creamy texture of Panna Cotta. It's an elegant and impressive treat for special occasions or whenever you crave a touch of indulgence.

www.ingramcontent.com/pod-product-compliance
Lightning Source LLC
LaVergne TN
LVHW061943070526
838199LV00060B/3956